Juneteenth
Celebration

Amanda Jackson Green

Consultant

Roy Rogers, Ed.D.
Principal, California

Publishing Credits

Rachelle Cracchiolo, M.S.Ed., *Publisher*
Emily R. Smith, M.A.Ed., *VP of Content Development*
Véronique Bos, *Creative Director*
Dona Herweck Rice, *Senior Content Manager*
Dani Neiley, *Associate Editor*
Fabiola Sepulveda, *Junior Art Director*
Luigi Savino, *Illustrator, pages 6–9*

Image Credits: cover Bastiaan Slabbers /iStock Photo; p3-4 Aaron of L.A. Photography/Shutterstock; p4 Tippman98x/Shutterstock; p5 Tippman98x/Shutterstock; p11 Keith Lance/Getty Images; p12 Sarin Images /Granger; p13 Granger; p14 North Wind Picture Archives/Granger; p15 Library of Congress [LC-DIG-cwpb-05697]; p16 Niday Picture Library/ Alamy Stock Photo; p17 Wikimedia Commons; p18 Alamy; p19 University of North Texas Libraries, The Portal to Texas History, https://texashistory. unt.edu; crediting Austin History Center, Austin Public Library.; p20 Library of Congress [LC-D401-18421]; p21 Jeffrey Isaac Greenberg 13+/Alamy Stock Photo; p22 Richard Levine/Alamy Stock Photo; p23 MediaNews Group/Reading Eagle via Getty Images; p24 White House; p25 Fort Worth Star-Telegram/Getty Images; p26-27 Associated Press

Library of Congress Cataloging-in-Publication Data

Names: Green, Amanda Jackson, 1988- author.
Title: Juneteenth celebration / Amanda Jackson Green.
Description: Huntington Beach, CA : Teacher Created Materials, [2022] | Includes index. | Audience: Grades 2-3 | Summary: "What is Juneteenth? Why do we celebrate this day each year? It is a day to recall the past. It is a day to honor freedom. In this book, learn the story of this U.S. holiday. Take a look at the people and customs that make it so special"-- Provided by publisher.
Identifiers: LCCN 2022010677 (print) | LCCN 2022010678 (ebook) | ISBN 9781087696225 (paperback) | ISBN 9781087696676 (ebook)
Subjects: LCSH: Juneteenth--Juvenile literature. | African Americans--Texas--History--Juvenile literature. | Slaves--Emancipation--United States--Juvenile literature. | African Americans--Anniversaries, etc.--Juvenile literature. | African Americans--Social life and customs--Juvenile literature.
Classification: LCC E185.93.T4 G737 2022 (print) | LCC E185.93.T4 (ebook) | DDC 394.263--dc23/eng/20220304
LC record available at https://lccn.loc.gov/2022010677
LC ebook record available at https://lccn.loc.gov/202201067

TCM
Teacher Created Materials

5482 Argosy Avenue
Huntington Beach, CA 92649
www.tcmpub.com

ISBN 978-1-0876-9622-5

© 2022 Teacher Created Materials, Inc.

Table of Contents

Freedom Day

Juneteenth is a **holiday** in the United States. It takes place each year on June 19. The name of the holiday comes from the date it honors. This is a mix of two words. The first word is *June*. The second word is *nineteenth*. Some people also call it Freedom Day.

A family celebrates Juneteenth.

What Makes a Holiday?

Some holidays, like Juneteenth, honor major events. Others are just for fun. For instance, the third Sunday in July is Ice Cream Day. Yum!

Some people wear clothing on Juneteenth that is inspired by African cultures.

JUMP INTO FICTION

Shout and Sing

It was a bright, humid day in Galveston, Texas. The morning was quiet. Ben was working in the corn fields. Sweat dripped down his face. Next to him, other enslaved workers moved in silence. Sometimes they talked or sang while they worked. But they were hot and tired.

Ben heard a loud voice in the distance.
He looked down the road.

A soldier on horseback yelled to the field workers, "I bring orders from the president. All people are free!"

At last! Slavery would end in Texas. All around Ben, people began to shout and sing.

BACK TO NONFICTION →

Good News Travels Slowly

Enslaved people in the United States fought to be free for more than 200 years. They met great danger along the way. But they kept pushing. Other people joined them.

A big change came in 1863. President Abraham Lincoln signed an order. He said enslaved people in some parts of the country must be freed.

This man is forced to work with no pay and in harsh conditions.

Law of the Land

Lincoln's order did not end slavery everywhere. It was the 13th Amendment a few years later that banned slavery in America. **Congress** passed that law in 1865.

It took a lot of time for the word to spread. There were no phones or internet. Soldiers traveled on horses to share the news.

Some **enslavers** hid the news. They did not want enslaved people to be free. They relied on forced workers to tend their **crops**.

News of freedom brings great relief and joy.

Enslaved people had to rely on others to tell them they were free.

Snail Mail

In the 1800s, letters traveled by horse or train. The trip from one town to the next could take many days or weeks!

At last, U.S. soldiers made it to Galveston, Texas. It was June 19, 1865. Two years had passed since the president gave his order. For the first time, thousands of enslaved people heard the good news. They were free. It was the start of a new life.

Some people are able to move away to start their new lives.

The Messenger

Gordon Granger was a soldier in the Union army. He is known for bringing the news of freedom to Texas.

The First Juneteenth

Celebrations broke out instantly. Newly freed people danced and sang. The day they had hoped and fought for had finally come! Families and friends met up to pray and **feast**. They did not know what the future would bring. But for that day, they were together. They were free!

People wear their best clothes to celebrate Juneteenth.

One Day, Many Names

Juneteenth goes by many names. Some call it Freedom Day. Others know it as Jubilee Day. People also call it Black Independence Day.

June
19
JUNETEENTH

A group of people celebrates Juneteenth in 1880.

In 1866, some Black Texans marked their first full year of freedom. June 19 was a special day for them. It was the first Juneteenth holiday. Freed people gathered for parties. Families dressed up in their best clothes. Some went to church, where they prayed and sang **hymns**.

This buggy is decorated for a Juneteenth parade.

Songs of Hope

Enslaved people often used music to pass the time while they worked. They sang about God, sadness, and their hopes for freedom. This music carried them forward into their new lives.

Many newly free Texans moved to other places. Some found jobs in other states. Others joined family members in the North. They honored Juneteenth in their new homes. The **custom** spread. New events popped up, too. Towns held parades. Churches had picnics. Big crowds met to hear leaders give speeches.

Hundreds of people gather for a Juneteenth parade.

Families and friends celebrate with good food.

Food Customs

Strawberry soda is a common drink at Juneteenth parties. Some hosts serve **red foods**, too. This might include red meats or red velvet cake.

The Tradition Grows

Texas leaders passed a law in 1980. The law made Juneteenth a state holiday. Other states joined them. By 2021, most states had laws like the one in Texas. Juneteenth may have started in Texas, but people in every state think it is a great day to honor.

Marchers celebrate in Harlem, New York.

June 19, 1865

Juneteenth Flag

Juneteenth has its own flag. The colors are red, white, and blue. The star in the middle honors Texas.

In 2021, U.S. leaders signed a new law. The law made Juneteenth a national holiday. Banks and post offices close for the day. Drum lines and dancers parade in the streets. People enjoy special foods and songs. It is a day for joy and rest. It is a day to honor freedom.

President Joe Biden signs the new law.

A Voice for Change

A woman named Opal Lee worked hard to teach people about Juneteenth. She pushed leaders to make it a holiday. She is known as the grandmother of Juneteenth.

From Past to Present

Juneteenth has grown a lot since 1865. Thousands of people honor the day each year. It is a day to remember the past. It is a day to give thanks for freedom. There are many ways to celebrate. Each one is special. That is because Juneteenth is special, too.

This mural shows the history of Juneteenth.

Freedom Walk

Galveston is home to the Freedom Walk. The trail marks the same path the soldiers took when they reached Texas in 1865.

Draw It!

Clothes can be a big part of holidays. On July 4, many Americans wear the colors of the U.S. flag. In India, people put on bold colors in honor of Diwali. Kilts are common at parties in Scotland.

What would you wear to a Juneteenth picnic? Create a Juneteenth T-shirt!

1. Draw a shirt outline.

2. Color the shirt with the colors that seem best to you for the holiday. Green, black, and yellow are often used to celebrate the holiday.

3. Add words if you like. You may also use symbols.

4. Share your shirt design with others. Tell them what it means to you.

Glossary

Congress—a group of people who make laws in the United States

crops—plants grown to be sold for money

custom—a practice that is common for a group of people

enslaved people—people who are forced to work without pay

enslavers—people who force other people to work without pay

feast—to eat large amounts of food

holiday—a special day of celebration

hymns—songs that praise God

red foods—holiday foods that are red in color and stand for the ancestors who suffered as enslaved people

Index

Your Turn!

There are all kinds of holidays. Some holidays honor people from the past. Some focus on special ideas. Write about the holiday you like most.

☆ What sets it apart from any other day?

☆ What do you do on this day?

☆ Are there certain foods you eat?

☆ What do you wear?